THE
YALE SERIES OF YOUNGER POETS

MANHATTAN PASTURES

AMS PRESS

NEW YORK

Volume 59 of the Yale Series of Younger Poets, edited by Dudley Fitts and published with aid from the Mary Cady Tew Memorial Fund.

Manhattan Pastures

SANDRA HOCHMAN

Foreword by Dudley Fitts

NEW HAVEN AND LONDON

Yale University Press, 1963

Library of Congress Cataloging in Publication Data

Hochman, Sandra.
  Manhattan pastures.

  Reprint of the ed. published by Yale University Press,
New Haven, which was issued as v. 59 of the Yale series of
younger poets.
  I. Title.   II. Series: The Yale series of younger poets ;
v. 59.
[PS3558.034M3   1976]   811'.5'4   75-21577
ISBN 0-404-53859-2

Copyright © 1963 by Yale University
Reprinted with permission of the original publisher, from the
edition of 1963, New Haven & London

First AMS edition published in 1976
Manufactured in the United States of America

International Standard Book Number:
Complete Set: 0-404-53800-2
Volume 59: 0-404-53859-2

AMS PRESS INC.
NEW YORK, N. Y. 10003

In Memory of Rose Schumer

Foreword

'With a Foreword,' says the Rubric, 'by the Editor.' And indeed there seems to be no considerable reason other than this liturgical one for an editorial prelude to the work of a new young poet. Looking back over my own exercises in this genre, and those of my predecessors, I am perplexed by a certain ambiguity of intention. Who is being served by the Foreword? The poet? Not really; he is his own best introduction, in his poems. The critic, then, or the ephemeral reviewer? One would not presume to think so. The general audience, whatever that may be? Possibly, though audiences happily have a way of neglecting Forewords; and in any event they would do better to begin with the poems. Yet ritual decorum must be observed, if for no other reason than that of custom, and the celebrant may at least combine invitation with his ceremony and so account in part for his personal intervention. I should like to discuss, very briefly and uncritically, what it was in Sandra Hochman's verse that persuaded me to choose it for this Series.

I liked its freshness, its generous delight in physical things, in textures and colors and odors, in the whole young experience of being alive. I liked the way in which a wealth of disparate objects was particularized and displayed, sometimes to be enjoyed for themselves alone, more often charged with a symbolic value. Thus the immediacy of contact in

the water
That flows down me, and to me, and from me,
Marl, turf, red earth, barbed root

which arrives at the queerly evocative stasis of the verses that first attracted me to Miss Hochman's work:

Surely the Khan of Tartary once dwelt
Beneath a tent of felt. O tent of felt!

Granted, quotation is not criticism; and for that matter, I am not sure what criticism could do with this couplet. The Khan of Tartary? Where did he come from? Not from Tartary, it would seem, but from Dante: at any rate, the title of the poem, 'Feltro e Feltro,' refers us to the first Canto of *Inferno;* but there the only Khan is Can Grande, and he is adducible only as an allusion, a possibility in a footnote. Miss Hochman's Khan, whoever he may be and whatever his provenience, most romantically resists explication; yet he is exactly right in being where and what he is in the poem, a barbaric aloof personification of physical freedom. The composition is calculated—coldly, I think, and with considerable audacity—, but I do not care about recovering the calculation. It is submerged in the odd grace of the poem, transcending footnotes.

I liked the ingenuousness of this writing at its best, a kind of urban-pastoral innocence. The intuitive, instinctual element in Miss Hochman's city eclogues is very strong, though it is almost always controlled, subservient to an ordering awareness. When it gets out of hand, as it infrequently does, the writing moves not so much in the direction of incoherence and obfuscation as towards a bemused picking up and putting down of more or less decorative objects, a dreamy catalogue in *recitativo*. Yet even this can be winning; and there are moments when overt rhetoric is persuasive against all expectation:

> Angel of meridian,
> Time out of the past,
> Lady fingers, broken strings,
> Unmade kisses in unmade bedrooms, unheld hands in
> Unkept closets, unsaid words to unknown lovers, unknown
> Movies in unknown dreams.

Soft, fluid, but incantatory again, and this time with no help from Tartary. The iteration and the paradoxes, the homeliness of the symbols, the very movement of the verse—these are all conscious, controlled, aware. Individually the elements may be personal *eidola,* and I suspect that often we cannot participate in the entirety of their emotional meaning; but there is nothing in the least ghostlike or specious in the art that deploys them to bring about so substantial an evocation of pleasure and guilt, of the loss and recovery of delight. The measure handsomely reflects the mood, most successfully, perhaps, in the elegiac dying-away:

> Lovers, when at last from sweet content
> You are caught in dreaming argument,
> You will drowse in grass
> Under the sea where swans are bound at last,
> Lovingly, lovingly.

But the amorous-melancholy is not the only vein, nor does Miss Hochman's unusual concern for muted effects divert her from the sharper issues. There is a sensible harsh wit at work here, too, and a comedic impulse that knows exactly the right way to bring the lyric back to earth. O tent of felt!

I find that I have been saying, with a repetitiousness that is perhaps not inappropriate in a baroque prelude, that I was first attracted to these poems by their honesty and by the visual and tactile quality of the writing. I do not mean to suggest that these are their only virtues, but they will serve as points of departure. And surely they are refreshing. No one subjected to new poetry in bulk, so to speak, can be unfamiliar with the for-print-only character of so much of it: the new formalism, with its ingenious metrical complexities that work only on paper; the post-beatnik ejaculations, sprawling or chopped, celebrating the self-adoration of ignorance; and, of course, the great welter of beauty-verse still, and for ever, entranced by the worst magic of the Georgians. But in Miss Hochman's work I find something more than a relief, grateful as that may be. An uncommon plainness, a willingness to take risks, a power to invest the ordinary with the strange, an amused (and amusing) control of the delicate forces of diction and of rhythm—these are what decided me, and they make up the sum of my accounting.

DUDLEY FITTS

Contents

CONTENTS

IVORY AND HORN

IN THE FLAME

About blood, I've my right hand in the sun. I burn
My hair, my name,
O, I have my God-hand at last in the fiery flame.
I enter light! (I have put on
The tennis sneakers of swift martyrdom) and
Run past palaces and pensiones,
Past lost hotels, public Italian johns,
Past the limp bodies of Acheron.
I never wanted to attract
Quick pinches of maniacs,
Selfish hands of flesh-mongers and quacks,
The selfish ones (always the ego cracks!),
I will go whoring with the Zodiac
And ride beyond
Deodorants, clean pillows and quilts,
The shared bath towel, the box of cleaning salts.
(This is not the heart of love that feasts
On someone's marriage sheets.)
Though flesh has held me with its feather fingers, I am gone.

Now I have my right hand in the sun.

Hell's a place
Where lover and beloved
Lip to lip face each other's crime. The man across my quilt
Turns quietly. I read of guilt,
I know guilt is a lie.
I dive
Into the water-bed of Charon,
Limbo dissolves my breath, Paolo and Francesca spin
Over my bed to comfort me.
When I turn against a night of restless
Sleep, my book and my beloved fall upon
The wind-stained willows of Acheron.

FELTRO E FELTRO

for Howard Nemerov

I have grown tired of the water-tap,
The bowing maids, the telephone messages, the crap.
From now on I will praise the water
That flows down me, and to me, and from me.
Marl, turf, red earth, barbed root
Are mint and sacrament.
Here is the household of the apple grass.
I know the kingdoms of the earth.
And I know the moon. One snowy owl
Jogs down from Canada.
Surely the Khan of Tartary once dwelt
Beneath a tent of felt. O tent of felt!

I.

I am locked in the kitchen, let me out.
Burning in the toaster,
Sizzling in the pan,
Choked in the gas range,
Iced in the kitchen glass,
Broken in the bowl,
I jump out of the cup.
Throw dish rags over my anger,
Crumbs over my head, anoint
Me for the marriage bed.
The bride is buttered, eaten when she's charred.
Her tiger falls into a tub of lard.

II.

Under a green comforter,
Waiting for love,
The heart of the city breaks
In my pillow, and down
The streets parade the cats
With wedding tails
And great plumed hats.

III.

Underneath the city
There is this: paws of a tiger.
For I have seen true dreams
Are white nights lit by black neon lamps.
I have seen the stripes
Of true and un-true dreams:
There are two gates of sleep; one of Horn
For true visions,
The other, shining, of white Ivory,
Through which ghosts
Send false dreams.

The bridegroom by himself is slain. Ivory
To Horn is chained.

IV.

I saw a kitten with a tiger's head
Chewing up nine lives. Dead
Sperm lice clinging to his catty snout,
He crawled back to the bag that let him out.
When you find the Tiger, kill him! they said.
I could not sleep. I walked about
New York and looked for him.
In the day time on the park's green lip I stood,
Blood in my mouth flowing like a stream of angry water.
Armed, at night, I ferried the East River,
And pounded on his door. The doorman came,
A blue lion tamer shooing off his game.

V.

Snow was falling the first day we walked
Along the river's edge. Rocks
Looking toward Welfare Island seemed a gift
Dropped out of a New England sailing ship.
Gulls followed us in the smoke undertow;
And eye for eye and tooth for tooth and eye for eye
My bridegroom slapped against the river's edge. The
Mayor's house was made of gingerbread.
I could not find the straight path out.

VI.

In Harlem
We climbed the movie steps
That led us to a market place of dance.
We watched a dark brown woman shake in two.
I am well, I move my arms, she said,
Never-never dreams wake up the dead.
At the Palladium
Dancing was praising.
Olive ladies
Moved their mattress bodies from the bed
And feather-danced their boys.
Over the wooden dance floor fell
A thousand moving pennies. Catch them all!
Swaying up and down,
No bodies touched, but all bobbed up and down
Jib-shaped and out of water.

I heard the prancing paws of the greased tiger.

VII.

We crossed Brooklyn Bridge.
In Brooklyn Heights
I heard the sacrament: *You said you meant—*
You said you meant—
Scaled the ice mountains. The
Tiger-eye was strange. I heard claws
Beating in the Stock Exchange.

VIII.

In the animal hospital:
Jaws of frightened animals. I looked at them,
Afraid to see the hairy cats completely shaved.

IX.

Near the tiger's bed, my eyes could see
Lovers dancing ceremoniously.
Gracefully, along the corridor,
Geese in slippers danced the varnished floor
Lovingly, lovingly.

On the white pallor of varnishing,
Lady-birds and clock-o-clays could sing.
Bees spun music on the chrome
Of a basin's sun waxed honeycomb
And jaguars pranced. A chittering toad
Sang to the blue eyes of a hog,
Lovingly.

Lovers, when at last from sweet content
You are caught in dreaming argument,
You will drowse in grass
Under the sea where swans are bound at last,
Lovingly, lovingly.

X.

I would like back my jungle gifts, as I now
Understand they were given on the basis of being
Deceived. These gifts are:

One white Mexican bird of peace,
One silver and glass treasure-box,
A golden ring,
My kaleidoscope,
One Japanese pen,
One Japanese ink grinder,
One Japanese scroll,
One small fan,
One book about the life of Mozart,
One red velvet crying pillow,
One picked-through book of Mallarmé,
One straw angel,
Two geraniums,
Two pink table cloths,
One white linen napkin,
Two small candle holders with peacocks on them,
Sugar-tongs,
A blue holy book for the Holidays.

That is all that is necessary for me to say to you
At the present moment. I hope you enjoy tearing
My white nightgown and my white toothbrush.

XI.

I woke and sucked my thumb. My room
Had melted into stones.
Bookcases filled with books were filled with stones.
The dresser drawer was saddled with a stone.
The telephone, all numbers, was a stone.
Uneven stones, inviting all contours,
Were varnished on my pillow.
Stones in the mirror. Cinnabar and stone.
You will find that I am
Ready for lapidation. I wept
And heard the bridegroom call my name.

XII.

Then Angel Lucifer walked the wall
Past the living-room and down the halls
Into my bedroom. He rocked
Me to his fables.

I laid me down to sleep and blurred
My eyes upon his cackling bird. We flew
Into the underworld. My arms
Stuck to his bird's crest, fingers curled
Around his wings. And I was borne
Over the gates of Ivory and Horn.

MANHATTAN PASTURES

On our wedding day we climbed the top
Of Mount Carmel. To keep our promises
We lay down in maize.
Who can tell us how to lead our lives?
Now in Manhattan's pastures I hear
Long processions of the compact cars
Nuzzling their gasoline.
The day is springtime. Have I come too late
To hear the Zen Professor speak of peace?—
One thing is as good as another, he says, and eats
Salad, wheat germ, and all natural foods.

Voices out of records: terrible sounds.
Wagner's music is a tongue.
My radio announces man in space. This
Was once my city. Who will tell us
How to lead our lives?

Eichmann stalls in the judicial stables.
His children saddle him to a black horse
Motoring through six million beds of grass.
He wears a light-wool suit tailored for summer.
The doctors say that we are doing well. We shall
Be cured of childhood if we keep
Counting our nightmares in the fields of sleep.
I shear black cars and records in my sleep.

Eichmann drops as man is shot in space
Out of a pop-gun. In our universe
A lonely husband needs a hundred wives. Who

Can tell us how to lead our lives?

HANSOMS

Never tame, those
Honey-speckled horses
That troupe through the streets of Manhattan
Prancing with jute saddles

Carrying dancers and opera bassos.
They lugged newspapers and dolls
To sad warehouses,
Clopped through the alleys of Broadway,
(Eyes riveted on neon meathooks)
They trotted to Harlem.
And met up with cab-drivers, blonde vegetable
Horses, and cornices, and veiled ponies
Adorned for the weddings of plazas. Then they ran
From the exile of parks
Past dummies, clothes-hooks, and pelts,
Trotting down Fifth Avenue
To the sea. They

Galloped on boats
Rode on the spokes of the tides,
Rode on Venetian gondolas,
Stayed close to the lotus sterns,
Rolled on cedarwood ships,
Returning from Thebes,
Galloped on Jason's glittering boat
Carved from the branch of Dodona,

They joined the oarsmen
Close to the axis, and sailed
With groups in the galley, sailed
Viking-ships beneath sea-masks,
Faced bulwarks and rowing benches,
Stamped hooves through gold bolts of damask. And cried
With their great yellow teeth while
Lateen sails swelled. They bit
The Roman merchants, traveled with dead-eyes,
Rammed against bulkheads.

They rode on the *Great Harry*
While leather shields were displayed,
Rode hulks and caravels, set their hinds
Against bowsprits. From Portugal
They set sail on the *Galleon*. They rode
On the *Voyage Armada,* froze on merchant's ships,
On flutes, on seventy-four gun ships, on luggers,
Bugalets, frigates, feluccas, and barques.
They leapt through their dreams on tartanes, burned
On xebecs and saïques,
Exiled on brigs, snows, brigantines until
Tamed by the sea, they came home.
Never broken. But they came home,
Home to the winter, home to saddle and crop,
Blanket, stall, and the whips
Of lovesick riders
Who drove them around and around
Central Park for a view of swans.

CONSTRUCTIONS: UPPER EAST SIDE

Wreckers
Drilling and breaking rock
As if New York were one great tooth
Rotten but smiling.
Gloria sits in her studio drilling and breaking boxes.
She is not setting foundations; she is making horses
Talk. She is dis-embalming dolls.
In Manhattan everything is being torn from rock.
Our buildings break. Even the ball,
The gong-ball destroying our buildings,
Breaks. Even tools
Built for destruction break.

Outside my window wreckers
Trapped in constructions: blond
And black men under helmets of steel, caught in earth. . .
Killing earth. The earth is taken somewhere else.
Where does all the earth go?
Wreckers in uniforms of mesh ride
Jackhammers and dust-machines, gripping
Torches of fire. They are precise. Sea shells,
The French horn, animal and vegetable are streamlined.

Drills,
The drills sound in my head. I toss words
Back at them. I throw them down as part
Of a new foundation.
I hang words over glass.

Who will escape
This tyranny of the T square?
Gloria, commissioned by
No-one, sets up her broken dolls.

Riding past mirrors and new office buildings,
She tries to construct
A small tower out of ivory and horn.
Dreams are nails. Her daydreams ring
On linoleum. Here, the man
Who dropped the bomb on Hiroshima, and went insane,
Grabs back his bomb again.
She's shrinking the jowl and the paunch of Diamond Jim Brady
To clean lines.
Glass is broken.

LIVING WITH VERMIN

Silverfish
Cling to each other.
Poets do not dare
Cart-wheel paths to the bedroom.
They crawl on the bathroom tile-ways
Where it is safe.

Their heritage will, no doubt, interest
Scholars and scientists,
Although it hardly interests my
Human foot. Which is what
They are afraid of:
                    They see it coming
And they crawl, scurrying
From a painted toenail.

Put them out of your night-mind,
But they keep circling patterns of the tile:
While you are warm in silent-movie dreams,
Artfully they enjoy the bathroom
Mistaking sinks and bathtubs
For sculpture. Slowly, they plumb
Your solar system.
Silver and black, their heads
Are camouflaged. But this is their protection:
They are more bashful than rodents.
Less beautiful than bedbugs.

Manhattan's
Small beasts, engendered
In corruption,
Fear for their lives.

Lower East
Side, Tower of Babel, pushcarts,
Temple of last year's newspapers covering
The world in shelters of odor,
Lost house, uncurled palace of broom—
Hair wrapped in curlers and braids,
It is you he feels in this gallery
Where plates hang sterilized, lobotomized
On fresh burlap walls, where penciled lines
Of human faces suffer under glass. It is you,
Tent of string and wash flapping towards
The east of Russia, the west of Vienna, he fears
Bobbing through the ice alps on a train, half insane
To reach the nowhere.

                    Beautiful dirt streets,
It is you he walked through in the drawing rooms
Of Paris, where delicate quartets
Played songs of no real Solomon. It is you
He was seeking in the coffins of Greek Islands
(Where everyone sought you), but found
Only red tomatoes walking out of a shoebox. In
The swallowed streets of Chios,
It was you he wanted. It was you in the drugged cafés,
In choked hotels, in mosques, in seas, in the yellow
Peeling bedspreads.

Filth streets, bread-spinning springs of our fathers,
We will sleep in you for ever.

I.

The Lord is my hospital.
Birth—in silence. Odd that I should fear
Green sheets and pillows everywhere.
An eyeless needle made me drink
Sacred rabbit's milk. Unsewn,
I sprang out of the family wound.
Grew and grew.

Once, in my girlhood, a fat man said
(His voice was wiped, his eyes were glass),
Please inspect the chloroform and
Winding sheets where we are born. Here in the clinic,
Parades a line-up of the dead.
Leather bells and hershey bars
Are, each day, so regular,
Here in the clinic, here, he said,
The dumb procession of the mad.

—odd that I should say
Not here! As if his hospital
Was made of veins, not stones
And earth and common beams.

II.

Beastly Babel of sleeping pills—
You, cast-iron men,
Make cathedrals out of hospitals.
Your women have made you will
Open skulls, lost genitals,
Broken spines, coated tongues—
Hell is all pillows.

III.

In the clinic:
When I was born airplanes
Above Manhattan General wrote
Injury and *Injured* in the sky.

Kingdom of bassinettes and bed, to
The faithless I say *Be born and die.*
                              And I returned,
Scared as a rabbit.

OBJECTS

for Denise Levertov

Snake-dancing down Greenwich Street, I'm aware of my shoes.
Every object stares, stares at itself like an eye
For sale. The Christmas Eye and the Hardware Eye
And the God Eye, all spill
Their pine needles threaded with snow,
Their figs and halavah immodestly covering each other,
Ropes and nails,
Yes, and the Vegetable Eye, lusty as an apple,
And the threaded eye of crosses.
Blinking at them all, I weep for the good eye!
      Objects frighten me.

Were it not for
These reptile shoes
That I follow—
Shoes pulling toward sewer fans,

Were it not for these reptile shoes
Hissing in front of me
Near the river front, breasted with fish,
I would not be dancing down Greenwich Street.
But I've come back
In black leather boots. (I remember seeing
Russian dancers at the Metropolitan
Clicking heels. I said to Arthur,
For all I know of God
He may be two tiny red leather boots clicking
One against the other.)
I'm walking down Greenwich street, lifted
Over water-wheel gutters by my toes.
Joy is in this street. As for the sage,
He stands without his shoes.

DIVORCE

New York. *Men are like cars,* Dolores
Turned on her bar-stool precariously
In Dylan's Bar, *When one goes by . . .*
Her finger pointed to the right
Directly parallel to her right shoulder,
As if to signal a dangerous turn,
Another comes along.
         STOP.
Locate her listener in a
Crash. White-walled wheels are torn.
Fenders smacked. Front lights and tail lights
Burn. The motor's on fire
As we signal *Help us! Let us out!*

Help. The white Ford
Consul's gone.
        CURVE.

Locate the driver. She wakes up
In a grease-papered hotel.
Hôtel de Londres. TURN. Alex
Gland, painter and ski champion (he says)
Once a mechanic in a Swiss garage
Now a meter-man, moves, white, nude, next to her, charges
In chug tones, *Women should not cry.* She signals
From her car-wrecked lips and lies: *Look. I'm not
Crying and I never cry. Men are like cars. When
One goes by . . .*
—*Like cars? Like Cadillacs?*—
*Another comes. No, that's not true, Alex.
You are like birds.*

Where Puerto Ricans
Squash seeds with ripe feet
And baby Hebrews dance to school,
Their curls
Dangling from manly suède hats,
I heard a voice
Singing clearly to me: *Don't*
Speak with men but with angels.

I dreamt of my dead grandfather
Who once lived on St. Mark's Place.
For a nickel he would minstrel
In the parks, or jostle hot dogs
On a wooden cart, not dreaming
That his sons could make a million.

My other grandfather plumbed most of Brooklyn.
He gave up plumbing for Show
Business. All the Broadway flops
Were hauled off in his trucks—

How can I bear to dig this warehouse up?
From now on
As I dog-step through
My city, I'll
        speak
Not to men but to angels.

We sing for the dead
Employed by *The Learned Society*.
The clerk files *heart* under the envelope
Meant for *eyes*, the bookkeeper enters
Human hair in her column of numbers,
The public relations expert exploits
Brains, the secretary types *s o u l s*
On white slabs of paper as the office
Boy feeds tubes to the copystat
And receives from his machine a collection
Of *teeth*. "Do you know
There's a dentist who claims the history
Of civilization is the history of human teeth
And all we know of ancient man
Comes right out of his jaw?" *H O. H O. H A W.*
H A W. Once I sang for the dead
At *The Learned Society*. I wailed
"*Good Morning*" in the human phone
With a singing voice less human,
As the president,
And his well-known assistant,
Called a meeting and gave grants
To lunatics and lunar assistants.

CLAY AND WATER

In my father's brickyard
I saw walls of brick around me. Bricks
Bricks, so bright they were,
One piled upon the other
Like small red suitcases left in the Gare St. Lazare.

I stood in my father's brickyard
And I wondered where I came from, or if
There was something I could ask him,
Something that we would not stumble on.
—Climbed to my father's office
Covered with white dust, there were files,
And a desk—and there! My father, curious
As I to know why I had come.
Then I asked him, *Tell me about bricks,*
Thinking that he certainly
Had something about bricks to tell me.
What is there to tell?—About bricks,
I insisted, *about their names.*
He looked through
Papers on his desk, all disarranged,
And asked Mr. Bard, his partner, who
Didn't know; and finding nothing to tell,
He said, *Bricks come from clay and water.*
They come from water and clay.

Later, when I walked into the yard,
I looked up and saw my father waving at me,
Standing like an old man
Cemented in the strong window.

One moment before flight, the seagulls long
To trade their perfect movement, and
I, in childhood, pitied them.
Salt tears cripple the wind. I walk
This standard island where mechanics rule
Dreams on an empty stencil. How we long
For movement in this landscape.

THE MAMMAL IN CAPTIVITY

I.

He wishes to be remembered
Not as someone who repeated
Observances. Not as a poet,
But as a husband. And when that failed,
A lover. And when that failed,
A tourist with a glass shield in his eyes
Who, for a nickel, took a cruise and saw
The skyline of Manhattan
Carved from blue cinder.
And when that fails,
He prefers to be remembered as a seal,
Simply a mammal who endured his life.
Captivity. Like one of those brown jokers
In the entrance to the zoo: clowning
A little, showing off, sunning, a flap
Of the arms, a lazy snooze, then dive
From rock to pool.
Having no alternative: happily tamed to do
What the mammal in captivity, to save
His skin, must do.

II.

Do not run to the nearest shelter. Awake.
Love is cawing. A particular white crow,
He opens his breast to fly. He dazzles
Us, then preens. Do not run for the nearest shelter.
Awake. For love's a
Black dove all this time. Hairy
And dull, he will hold anything
Between his claws
Preening and devouring our mornings.

III.

This should have been our mornings:
Energetic and believable. Sky
Above our city scratched with beasts,
Ground coffee before speaking. Books
On the tables. Cool water and soap,
And little to be eaten. (Fruit sellers
Scurrying in the streets.) Dressing, working,
Answering the doorbell.
Cleaning. Dusting. Dying.
Then re-birth in the market!
Hoyden things! A hookah pipe, mixture
Of melons, artichokes, sausages, fruit
In every form—rectangles and circles—
Honey with a spine of wax. Fish
In a ribbon catch. Dried onions
And peppers dangling on a line. Centuries
Of cheese spilling milk.

I hear you, like a tame seal,
Barking on a xylophone
Your theme song: *Let me*
Be free one more morning.

RIVERSIDE DRIVE

I.

Women who are not alive
tame from the hearth and ashen husbandry
cluster on the Drive
while sun slips in their eyes
to be forgotten there. They never rise
from silence on their bench, but ache to whine
or jump to see the Hudson
shine her olive fingers on the walls.
Even a child's plaything—
a golden hoop—
will pass their breasts as if they were not women.
Once, they were known to frighten men of Greece
back home. In search of sexless peace.

II.

Crossing the Drive
The nurse told her future: *When you grow up
You'll be a baboon.*

Her parents pretended they were not happy
Piled up like rowboats lying on their sides
And picked themselves up for new boats and correspondents
And she saw
Many boarding schools. And dreamt of tugboats.

Later still, sun. And a kidnap:
Nothing is as important as a pencil. Write this down.

At that moment
Saved by the boy scouts who happened
To be marching in the hills during
Her kidnap. New correspondences
And college. And a battered man, a quack in a hotel

Room saying *When I write*
I never put all my eggs in one basket. Voyages. Birds
Wore tweed flat hats with tiny beaks.
She stared, that year, at jawfuls of the sun.

I.

Suddenly
I am discharged from my job
In a dream of numbers. Coins
Hiss. This is Wall Street: gold
Bricks glitter. There was a salmon
In a pack of bills, remember?
Within the files
Mr. Frank Organ, chief of the department,
Said, *It is the most important section of the Bank*
When people need it. When people don't need it,
It is the most forgotten. All written material,
Memoranda, papers, slips, checks, scribbles,
Are kept for at least thirty years.
Mr. Organ supervises over 30,000 boxes
Of records. None of them get away.
Look here, Mr. Organ, how the sea glitters!
Bank of Banks. Goodbye to your coin shelters.

Women, mostly fat,
Mopped the ladies' room,
And underneath the rest room,
Beyond the guards holding guns
Like real cops without robbers,
Men were burning money.
They worked hard, all day, burning money,
Shoveling it into vats.
Upstairs, a man took a photograph
In the photograph cubicle. Painters
Carpenters, cabinet makers,
Money counters, women sorting checks,
Women in the Health Department
And in the Foreign Department,
And Retirement Counselors,
And Personnel Counselors,
And Receptionists,
Sat above the flames. Arithmetic
Went on through the bars.

Beginning tomorrow, elevator
Men, carpenters, new employees,
Will have their fingerprints checked.
Everyone will be inspected before leaving
The Bank of Banks.

I alone have escaped with this poem.

A farm. A cannon on a hill.
Long ago I sat beneath that cannon
And picked clover. Often, at sunset,
I walked down to the barn, and held my arm
Around a calf, or took the one-eyed pony for a ride.
Later, I walked in the forests of corn.
The stalks were palm-boughs, strands of yellow sun.
Evenings, I picked tomato vines.
Earth clung to them, they prickled in my hand.
And our house was always lit. My grandfather
Furnished it from his *Broadway Theatrical Warehouse.*
Everything only seemed to be what it was: cupboards
Didn't open, prop tables had three sides,
Books were cardboard thick, lamps dimmed on,
Statuettes were paper silhouettes—
Papier-maché, they seemed to have no weight upon the farm.
Even the cannon had come home
From a play about war. It had been in
A smash hit in which Nazis, like
Chippewas, lost. There it stood,
Up on our hill, made out of wood,
Soggy and warping from the summer rain.

Cannon Hill Farm was sold. Black
Out. Nothing works but a kitchen knife.

MOSAICS

We clawed through Paris
And said, "Let's be alone
And talk to the dead." We spoke to Baudelaire.
Good morning,
Hookers are gone,
Artists are all over Montparnasse
Tinkering with fenders and ice-boxes,
Creating statues
That destroy themselves.
Good morning, grunted Baudelaire,
How are the ragpickers? The lesbians? The vampires?
Only art is left, we said.
And the poets?
Dead.
And the hellcats? The dangerous girls? The children
Tearing maps? The hangmen? The carrion boys
Swinging in the belfry of their bones?
All gone.
And what about the tears of snow? The
Scratching virgins? The libertines?
They pose for PARIS MATCH, we said.
Paris is dead.

My
father
dreams
that I
shall be
a wife.

Setting me
up in weeds
outside a
house where
beds of flowers
plunge
into fertilizer (he
would plant
me there)
with greenish braids
veined on my
ivory neck
twisted above
blood-checked gingham
in a knot
of love.

All his tears
fall from
his glassy rimmed
spectacles
to awaken him.

Father, sleep
in Jerusalem.
I hate
the plastic
fixtures
in this place
where we
erase
my childhood. For
a house
is where
deep
purposes are
broken
off.

ARCHIPELAGO

This is no Cannibal Isle
Merely the smile of the toad,
Merely the gates shining white in the sun
On the rocks of this virginless isle.

Orange trees, the coconut, the palm
Would tear the eyes out of an Englishman
If he
      dared
          to go
             into the
ARCHIPELAGO!

Orange trees? And coconuts? And palms?
Come, stalk with me through a wilderness of worms.
Jump on a Partridge!
Jump on a Pelagic Confervae Infusoria (Anima
Extroria)
While the spider with an unsymmetrical web
Offers us a widow's pain.
Jump on your name!

Shame on the Archipelago. *Shame* on the Archipelago.
Shame. Shame.

Let us fall from pride awhile, sip
Bile of a waterfrog, riverhog, jaguar,
Kingfish and parrot. Stamp
Through peat
And eat cheap with the birds,
Eat cheap.

Down the stream of lava,
Down the stream of penguin-stone

Home is the Archipelago. Home is the Archipelago. Home.
Shall we excur
          Shall we excursion to

Colonial del Sacramento, Santa Cruz, Valparaiso,
P A R A D I S E ?
They won't tell you
That the sagacity of mules is unlike the "ignorance of savages."
They won't tell you of heavy rain today,
Strange noise of butterflies, and worms. This is no
Shell. But orange trees,
And coconuts,
And palms
Scratch the eyes out of an Englishman.

1. *Where is Orpheus?*

> *Where is Orpheus?*
> *Where is Christ?*
> They have gone
> Into icons. And song.
> Into halls of mosaic,
> Into the rot of cherrystone and rock.
> I come into the museum of Byzantium
> Lip to lap
> With gods and face
> Their portraits.
> *Where is Orpheus?*
> *Where is Christ?*
> Speak!
> They look down
> From icon frames.
> Christ smiles.
> Orpheus finds his lyre.
> Speak. But all the children
> Stand dumb in the hallways.

II. *Simon Says*

Simon says *Love serves to be greedy.*
Take giant steps. *Love serves to be free.*

Bluff. Love is a bandage. Change it each
Seven years. Blind the old skin. Change it.
Love when it hurts, heals. An umbrella step:
Love blind. Fall deep in. Drown.

Step. Give your world away.
Stand still. Move. Spin. *Take little steps,*
Says Simon who will never see.
You are out! That's what Simon says.

THE PARIS ACROPOLIS

—36 Rue de Lille

Arms, hooves,
Amputated, floating on
The walls, as they might appear in a dream.

Subletting the gargantuan
Paris apartment of Madame
Foumenille—36 Rue de Lille—
We were visitors in her bedroom. What
Surprised us were murals
Running in a film of white paint:
Naked men and women clustered on her walls
Enjoying each other in a bacchanal.
Caught on the wall, without embarrassment,
Protruding male organs, buttocks,
Exaggerated breasts, dismembered heads
Of—the happy
Greeks—the gods!
By our bed,
A naked man popped out of an oyster shell.
Over the fireplace, great
Horses, open-mouthed, with open-mouthed foam,

Ears flattened to their manes, devoured
Polite virgins. The furniture
Raised unnecessary hurdles
For goddesses. The horse-men
Had them all.
The photographs
On Madame Foumenille's dresser
Stared at the walls. Watching the Greek
Seduction from his faded icon frame, a Russian general
Stuffed his moustache flat against the glass;
Caught in his deva uniform,
He blushed, tipsy and aghast, agonized
By withered gods and goddesses. Our galloping white horses.

ADAM

Dripping winters
Peer from wood-work in this fake Sistine,
Watch my muscles stretch,
My fingers rest upon the looking-glass
Gripping suspect figures.
Adam in the mirror. Who am I?
I have not died, but I have seen my soul
Plunge from ceiling to the bedroom wall,
And so, when I say *death*, I mean each time
I've loved, and could not love, each time I've wept
And could not reach for something which leapt
Over *death*

Opening up the looking-glass again.

This black knight inhabits me. He stands
Stark as iron sculpture. Truly, he is made
Of wood as tough as iron. I had thought
Of taking him, my ancient foe, who wins
By standing where my sex begins.
I'll capture him. I'll take him down
From his check-mate of blood. My blood. But he has won.

Venice, you are not
The image of Narcissus in the water,
Not a coffee pot boiling
For a delicate rich finger. You are
Glass (not the beads,
Nor the necklace, nor the ashtray,
Nor the ugly cupids playing with
Themselves), but you are glass
Out of the fire, discarded on a beach,
The surplus of all that is not useful.

And in Venice I play with words.
I say *Venice the Menace* and walk through gardens
Of alabaster weeds. I say *Venice is Venus* and stroke
Angels who twirl around clocks. I say
Gondola and say *Canal*
And shout *Giudecca*.

                    Once there was a Venetian,
Blind. Blind as a blind could be. She woke up
In the afternoon reciting poetry. And walked down the streets,
And fell into a canal, singing *I am so damn
Blind I can't see God at all.*

Angel of meridian,

Time out of the past,
Lady fingers, broken strings,
Unmade kisses in unmade bedrooms, unheld hands in
Unkept closets, unsaid words to unknown lovers, unknown
Movies in unknown dreams.

Once,

I dreamt through a window over the Hudson,
I dreamt of the Palisades over the window,
The window on the one hand,
The Paradise on the other. And words

Floating glass from water.

I. Song of Years

> Years wear us
> Down. Quartered in our room
> I hear my wife trot to the dining room
> Setting her table while I plan my day.
> This morning is Spring. The sun is out.
> My grandchild's in the park with other foes
> Who ride with him and bind him secretly
> To ancient games of chivalry—
> Our day is played. My enemy calls
> For battle. Or for breakfast. I rise,
> Trot, wait beneath the cressets of our stove
> To feed her with my love.

II. Revelations

> One afternoon in the Egyptian zoo
> Two swans arrived.
> I watched them float silently.
>
> The feathers of one swan had changed
> To a copperhead's green scales.
> I saw the slanted eyes,
> The open tongue,
> Become the swan's slant eyes.
>
> Swans into white serpents changed.

III. The Master

My only pupil met me in the city
And we spent one afternoon together
Hid from the scrutiny of summer
In a quiet park.

Stuffed in the hub of the universe
She spoke of adolescence, I, of verse.

What was first obscure, rippled
As clear as water around us,
As leaves.

And when the white moon came,
Cracking day and night,

We found the subway station
For her train. She took the universe,
I waved goodbye.

I am hungry for the bakeries, not
Their bread. I am hungry for the road
That ran through every country,
And the tree turning color from the south
Up to the north. I am hungry for the salt,
Famished for the shields of odor,
Flags of color, but I will not eat.

Flesh, you are going.
Having given up the taste for meat,
I have given up the taste for fruit.
I have given up the taste for cheese. Salads
And weeds do not tempt me. Thirst is gone.

—but I'll never find him.
I'll open my bed for a secret. And
Hang up my clothes.
Become an old woman in three days.

LOVE-FAST II

I turn a song of rooms,
My pages are white ceilings filled with light.
Of all the things inside my room,
The oak working table, and the bed,
The books and records, pictures, of it all
By far the most beautiful
Is the black music stand.

The room drifts back
Into the black iron music stand.

DAVID

He lay with his head full of psalms
Wondering how a boy
Could shed his mind
And kill a giant.
The battle was set. All the dark
Night he lay
Facing the stars and God.

Am I to die?
My mind is caught in the strings
I touched as a child,
They will not let me arm.
How shall I begin
To think of the battle, a way
To fight?
His songs remained
And kept him company.

When the armies were set, and
Goliath stood in that place
Where he knew the battle must be,
David turned all songs to a stone
And overthrew the flesh.

GRIEF

I.

A fireman enters. He entertains us
With his water-gun, struts around the building,
Warns us not to "use the incinerator."
"What shall we use?"
The fireman enters the flame,
The buildings burn. He waves inside the ruins.

II.

I placed inside my hair,
After the flames,
Three peacock feathers, each
With a perfect quill.
I know they will change with the color of morning light
As eyes take on new colors when we cry.
I placed inside my hair
A new eyesight. The peacock walks my forehead as I lie
Alone.

III.

Grief enters new cities on
A match-stick.
Grief's in the garage, Grief's in
The windshield; Grief
Is the fireman.

THE DIAMOND NEEDLE

After she left
With long-
Playing phonograph records,
She took another look,
And finding nothing,
                            escaped.

She carried her notes.
And they spoke back,
Like the Duckbill Platypus
Under her arm, with an ancient
Quack, Quack, this secret language
Placed in the past
Beyond time and origin, a skin
Stretched out, or a name
That, after all, was her own.

On the way, she realized, with
Some alarm, that she had forgotten
The diamond needle it was
To be played back on.

Sneaking back to the Prodigal
Country, in the guise of an animal,
She wrenched the needle from the mechanical
Arm of a phonograph marked
Property of the Library of Congress
United States Government,
Division for the Blind.

The needle was perfect, though used before
By someone who had stopped there.
She glanced at the library's
Vault, a great machine
That played with time and space. Voices
Of the writers of her time
Were kept there in capsules, like diet pills
Called *Bestiana* or *Preludin,* very desirable
For taking off weight, or like those tiny capsules
Of hair color that turn gray hair yellow
When broken on the head after shampoo.

These notes (she read)

Will remain. Unopened
For the millennium.

DIVERS

We have chosen the sea
Because we are lonely
And resemble
All things that go down.
Sucking the sun
In our silver-finned sea-chests,
We leave antennae touching the sky,
We plummet
In the great hives of water.
Che farà Euridice?

Go, bleed the waves
And find the blue jail of Euridice.
The sea-blades wind her fingers in the salt.

(There is no bottom chamber to the sea.)
Find on the tips of waves that drifting face.

THE DEATH OF JOAN

In the ice-box infirmary
Everything is white.
Now and then
A woman saint is born. Foundress of nothing,
She sobs after unattained goodness,
Burns in her weariness,
Trembles among the fever trees,
Squats all morning,
Suffering for the long recognizable deed,
Sees berry bushes on The Commons bleed.

In the college infirmary
You, Joan, were a wild woman Cossack
Re-reading *Anna Karenina*
And chewing on a little ball of fur.

I read: *St. Theresa, a child beast, went out for a walk.*
She walked with her brothers into the country of moors.

Saints are through, you said.

I said: *St. Theresa's passionate nature*
Demanded an epic life.

So does everyone's, you said,
And I'll take my life.

Joan   Joan   Joan

I.

    "Doctor, voices appear to me in forms
Human and desperate, each in its own body
Bending, running tip-toe on a screen
As if in bed. *Do you know what I mean?*
Sounds in cushions, silent-movie frames,
Words, naked in Alphabet: alphabet forms:
Y's and W's open-armed,
I's and B's kissing with huge lips—
The camera shifts to J's and B's as black R
Clinches white.
          Doctor,
I'd like to be a film-maker
Shooting naked letters—hidden under
The pillow, through a mesh of swan
And ticking—caught, you know, by the arm:
Close up. But there is nothing new—
Silence, and leisure—"

II.

"In solitude one knows the maxims of the body:
Neon light—over the belly—
The first maxim:

If you cannot love
Unhook your arms.

Lit by a flashlight:

If you cannot love
Unhook your head."

III.

She sleeps in a bed
Of sweat
Completely vertical
Wondering how things
Will turn out at her funeral. Her
Death is simple and unfortunate.

This was her diary as a virgin:
"Reading the life of Anna Pavlova
Studiously in the tub,
I wonder if love is the same sensation
As the bathwater's flowing motion."

My love after a long journey comes home.
Wrists of time move as they moved before,
Time pounds on the window and pounds again
And what seems like time is only the rain.
Left with our harvest of salad and Greek vermouth
We hide in the kitchen. An ivory snake's tooth
Is in the kitchen stove, and cubes of ice;
Dinner is all we have left of Paradise.
Adam and Eve inside us died,
Angry shadows on the window pane.
I scrape death from the black spots of a radish.

It's all mosaics now:
Blue socks, yellow shirts, brown slacks,
Blonde hair, the oriental lamp
That came from Turkey inside out.
It's all mosaics now:
Orange socks, argyle hats,
Blue jackets, green slips,
Brown trousers lined with stripes,
Give me the coral jacket I gave you.
Tonight it's a red coat and a black comb,
And a fan, and?
Velvet hats, yellow broom,
Pink cleaning rags,
Purple kitchen,
Yellow bird,
All our separations are colors.

Street in Paris,
Streets in Rome,
"I'm always safe under your arm." Gray
Shoes, green scarf,
"I'm going to look for a newspaper and . . ."
"What is it you've got on?"
It's all mosaics now.

EROS AND HER BROTHER

—5 Rue d'Alger

Eros and her brother lived
In a house that was not a house,
Slept in a bed
That was not a bed,
Found a maid that was not a maid
But a monster called Agapé.

And they lived this way: Agapé
Wore black skirts, white aprons
Stiff as linoleum, and collected American
Stamps from Eros. Agapé preferred stamps
With white portraits of Abraham Lincoln
Pressed like a cameo against a pink background
And took

Stamps home to her chamber of maids
Where she cared for two children of her
Own. *Look, children!* she would say in Great
French, and they would press the stamps
Against their foreheads and pretend
They were sending themselves to America.

Eros and her brother, who was not
Her brother but her husband, could not

Sleep. Eros awoke and said, *Listen! I hear*
A terrible noise in my love-ear. Outside
Our window there's a fallout of
atoms, airplanes, automobiles,
And clanging ashcans. (Everything deadly

Began with an A.) After that,
The cave blew up. Agapé collected her stamps
And ran home. The bed rocked to splinters
And out of the splinters rolled Eros
And her brother. Rolled into the street. Out
Of the street into the earth. *Merde!*
Screamed Agapé. *I feel the loneliness of*
Their dreams in mine.

THE HAIRBRUSH

In the end
There will be nothing but a hairbrush.
I shall find the bristles to be soft. Brush
My hair, and with my hair my mind
And unknown cavities of water.
I shall brush and tease. Until pools of memory
Are like all strands of hair: soft,
So clean, or singed.